Nirguṇa Mānasa Pūja

Worship of the Attributeless One in the Mind

by

Śri Śaṅkara

Translated into English by

Dr. H. Ramamoorthy

Assisted by

Master Nome

Published by
Society of Abidance in Truth
1834 Ocean Street
P.O. Box 8080
Santa Cruz, California 95060
USA

Foreword

The great Indian Sage, Śri Śaṅkara, disciple of Śri Govindapada in the lineage of Śri Gaudapada, realized the Absolute Truth at a young age and with his journeys brought new life to the non-dual teaching of Advaita Vedanta. Though many centuries have passed since his youthful years of teaching, the works of Śri Śaṅkara still epitomize the central truth of Advaita Vedanta and the various approaches to it. In addition to numerous sacred texts, the Sage established four major centers which thrive to this day, along with innumerable other ashrams throughout India. One of the scriptural gems left in this rich spiritual heritage is the present work, *Nirguṇa Mānasa Pūja (Worship of the Attributeless One in the Mind),* in which Śaṅkara's verses apply the highest non-dual interpretation to ritual worship, and at the same time elevate the significance of the pūja items with the very highest, non-dual interpretations.

Building upon symbolism already known to those familiar with devotional pūja worship, Śri Śaṅkara expounded non-dual interpretations to reveal for the devotee, who is a disciple, a deep inner meaning for each aspect of the ritual. Linking in this way devotion and wisdom, the great Sage also facilitated retention of the teaching through the correspondence of pūja practices and non-dual principles.

This unique and precious text was translated from Sanskrit with the benefit of considerable experience and scholarship brought to the effort by Dr. H. Ramamoorthy. Collaborating with the translator was Master Nome, who composed the introduction that follows and also provided ongoing spiritual insight for rendering this present form most beneficial to sincere lovers of Truth who seek the spiritual treasure contained here.

The Society of Abidance in Truth is happy and truly blessed with the opportunity to offer for the first time in English this succinct non-dual treatise by Adi Saṅkara. Under the guidance of Master Nome, the Society of Abidance in Truth makes available, in holy texts and Satsang, the non-dual teaching of Advaita Vedanta as taught by Sri Ramana Maharshi and Sri Saṅkara. All who are interested in Advaita Vedanta or Sri Ramana Maharshi, who wish to visit the Society or obtain books containing this Teaching and literature about the Maharshi, as well as all who are interested in supporting or furthering the Society's efforts to publish the sacred, treasured texts of this Teaching, are warmly invited to contact the Society. The Society especially wishes to express profound appreciation for the fine, dedicated work of Dr. H. Ramamoorthy and to acknowledge his inspiring approach to this project. We also thank the numerous spiritual aspirants whose selfless efforts contributed to this publication, and we remain ever grateful for the great Sages who shine the light of highest Knowledge for all to see.

The Publisher
(Board of Directors,
Society of Abidance in Truth)

Contents

Introduction

OM

Obeisance to Adi Śaṅkara, who is Śiva, who is unalloyed Being-Consciousness-Bliss, who abides as the one Self, who reveals the non-dual Truth, expounding the clearest Advaita Vedanta, who irrefutably proves the utter identity of Atman and Brahman, whose spiritual glory is ineffable, and who Liberates from all bondage those who seek the Knowledge with which he shines.

Obeisance to Bhagavan Śri Ramana Maharshi, who is Siva, who is unalloyed Being-Consciousness-Bliss, who abides as the one Self, who reveals the non-dual Truth, eloquently expounding the clearest Advaita Vedanta in speech and Silence, who irrefutably proves the Truth that the Self alone is and is Brahman, whose spiritual glory is ineffable, who is my ever-gracious Guru, and who unfailingly puts to an end all of the imagined bondage.

The *Nirguṇa Mānasa Pūja,* or *Worship of the Attributeless One in the Mind,* is intended for them who are desirous of abiding in the non-dual Truth. It reveals the highest form of worship to be the state of identity with the formless Absolute. That state in which the Absolute and the Self are undifferentiated, in which all misidentification and duality have ceased, is the natural state of Self-Realization.

All beings offer worship. Some people worship such illusory concepts as the belief in an ego entity, the belief in a differentiated mind, the delusion of the "I-am-the-body" notion, and the ignorant notion of an existent world. Wise aspirants, according to their understanding, worship God and Guru. The Maharshi states, "When he reaches a certain stage and becomes fit for enlightenment, the same God whom he was worshipping comes as Guru and leads him on. That Guru comes only to tell him, 'That God is within yourself. Dive within and realize.' God, Guru, and the Self are the same."[1] The more their understanding is free from delusive notions, the more profound and blissful is their worship. It is said, "What one worships, one becomes." Worship results in merger or union.

When one abandons all delusive notions, inclusive of the individual (ego) 'I' to which all the other notions pertain, the highest worship results. This is worship of That which is all-transcendent, yet ever present. It is the worship or pūja of the Self, which is completely attributeless and qualityless (nirguṇa). One then sees that all worship is simply a means of perceiving That which is beyond all perception and conception. The Maharshi declares, "Under what-

---

[1] Mudaliar, A Devaraja, ed. *Gems from Bhagavan.* 2nd ed. Tiruvannamalai, South India: Sri Ramanasramam, 1969. p. 26.

ever name and form one worships That which has no name or form, it is only a means of perceiving it."[2] That is the Self. The perpetual pūja or worship of the enlightened is this nirguṇa pūja, which is described in this wondrous scripture composed by Śri Śaṅkara.

In this dialogue composed by Śri Śaṅkara, the one Self appearing as the Guru explains this supreme worship of abidance in and as the one Self to the same Self appearing as the disciple. From the onset, the disciple's stand is quite formless, and the verses describing his questions bear a close resemblance to the great Sage Ribhu's declarations in verses 27 through 31 of chapter three of the *Ribhu Gita,*[3] which describes the worship of the linga of the Supreme Self. The Guru responds with the description of pūja to the linga of the Self in terms that again resemble the *Ribhu Gita,* chapter three, verses 32 through 41. This pūja to the formless Self is the pūja to the Supreme Śiva, Brahman. Abidance, free of illusion, in and as the Self—Brahman, Śiva—of the nature of Being-Consciousness-Bliss, is the quintessence of this worship.

Advaita, or Non-duality, is the Truth. This Teaching of Non-duality, Advaita Vedanta, is the revelation of what is—Reality. Reality is one only. It is utterly formless and free of creation and destruction. The Self alone exists. It is Brahman. It is Śiva. There is not even a possibility of a trace of anything else, ever.

The Self-Realized Sage knows this complete identity of Śiva—the Absolute—and the Self. Being's timeless

---

[2] Osborne, Arthur, ed. "Reality in Forty Verses," verse 8. *Collected Works of Sri Ramana Maharshi,* 3rd ed. Tiruvannamalai, South India: Sri Ramanasramam, 1968. p. 117.

[3] Tamil rendering of *Ribhu Gita.*

repose in itself, free of all differentiation, is the supreme, attributeless worship. This is the perpetual worship of the enlightened.

Spiritual aspirants should approach this *Nirguṇa Mānasa Pūja* with a heart full of sincerity and devotion, with an ardent desire for Liberation, and with an introverted mind. They should approach with nonattachment toward all that is transitory, is objective, has beginning or end, is dependent upon the senses or the mind, or that is contained within the waking, dreaming, or deep sleep states of mind. They should approach this formless pūja with humility. They should approach with the understanding that the Self is not the ego and that the latter is unreal. They should approach this formless pūja, eager for Self-Knowledge, free from delusive concepts, in a manner that results in merger with the Supreme. They should approach with the firm conviction that reality is the one Absolute alone, and, realizing that they are That, abide in unending Bliss.

By reading and meditating upon these illuminative verses by Adi Śaṅkara, one will experience this profound, supreme pūja. Both those who engage in the practice of the outward performance of pūja and those who do not will be greatly benefitted and illumined by this gracious, wise teaching of Śri Śaṅkara. May all who read these sacred lines be liberated from vasanas (tendencies) and bondage, be immersed in blissful Self-Knowledge, and be ever absorbed in perpetual worship in the blemishless, space-like temple of pure Being, the Self.

~ Master Nome

Scheme of Transliteration

Vowels:

अ	इ	उ	ऋ	ऌ
a	i	u	r	l
आ	ई	ऊ	ॠ	
ā	ī	ū	r̄	
ए	ओ			
e	o			
ऐ	औ			
ai	au			

Consonants:

क	ख	ग	घ	ङ	
ka	kha	ga	gha	ṅa	
च	छ	ज	झ	ञ	
ca	cha	ja	jha	ña	
ट	ठ	ड	ढ	ण	
ṭa	ṭha	ḍa	ḍha	na	
त	थ	द	ध	न	
ta	tha	da	dha	na	
प	फ	ब	भ	म	
pa	pha	ba	bha	ma	
य	र	ल	व		
ya	ra	la	va		
श	ष	स	ह	क्ष	ज्ञ
śa	ṣa	sa	ha	kṣa	jña

Notes on Transliteration

The following may be specially noted under consonants:

The Sanskrit letters shown are actually the consonant plus the vowel **a**; e.g., **ka** is the consonant **k** plus vowel **a**. The consonant alone will be represented in Sanskrit thus: **k** = क् i.e., with a (्) below the letter.

The second column and fourth column of consonants are aspirated sounds, or harder sounds, of the first and third columns denoted by the addition of **h**.

The fifth column gives the nasal sounds relating to the preceding consonants in the same line. e.g.,

ṅ for **k, kh, g, gh** **ñ** for **c, ch, j, jh**

ṇ for **t, th, d, dh** **n** for **t, th, d, dh**

m for **p, ph, b, bh**

The letter **c** represents the sound usually denoted in English words by **ch**.

The **ch** in the scheme of transliteration is equivalent to a sound represented by **chh** in usual English writing.

The difference in sounds between **ṭ** with a dot below and **t** without a dot, as also **ḍ** with a dot below and **d** without a dot, is to be noted; likewise the difference between **ṭh** with a dot below **ṭ**, as also **ḍh** with a dot below **ḍ**. The sounds are given on page xii.

The sounds **ṅ**, **ñ**, and **ṇ** are also given on page xii.

The sounds **s**, **ṣ**, and **ś**, respectively represent the sounds denoted in normal English writing by **s** = s, **ṣ** = sh, and **ś** = intermediate between **s** and **sh** (as in Śaṅkara, Śiva).

The letter **ṁ** with a dot above, in most cases will have the same sound as **m**, but where **ṁ** with dot above occurs in the middle of a word, it has to be pronounced as the nasal sound of the category of consonants following: e.g.,

Śaṁkara as Śaṅkara (**ṅ** for **k** category)
Śaṁkalpa as Śaṅkalpa (**ṅ** for **k** category)
Kiṁcit as Kiñcit (**ñ** for **c** category)
Saṁcita as Sañcita (**ñ** for **c** category)
Ghaṁṭa as Ghaṇṭa (**ṇ** for **ṭ** category)
Paṁḍita as Paṇḍita (**ṇ** for **ṭ** category)
Śāṁtiḥ as Sāntiḥ (**n** for **t** category)
Skaṁda as Skanda (**n** for **t** category)
Śaṁbhu as Śambhu (**m** for **p** category)

ṁ with dot above at the end of a word or end of a line of stanza can be pronounced the same as **m**.

ḥ with dot below called visarga usually occurs at the end of a word. It is then pronounced like **h** with a suitable short vowel sound following, e.g.,

aḥ or **āh** as **aha** or **āha**
iḥ or **īh** as **ihi** or **īhi**
uḥ or **ūh** as **uhu** or **ūhu**
e as **ehe** **ai** as **aihi**
o as **oho** **au** as **auhu**

अ	a	like *u* in sun
आ	ā	like *a* in ah!
इ	i	like *e* in reform
ई	ī	like *ee* in peel
उ	u	like *u* in pull
ऊ	ū	like *oo* in pool
ऋ	r	between *ri* and *ru*
ॠ	ṝ	*ṛ* elongated
ऌ	ḷ	between *li* and *lu*
ए	e	like *a* in pale
ऐ	ai	like *i* in sigh
ओ	o	like *o* in pole
औ	au	like *ow* in prowl
क	k	as in book
ख	kh	*k* above aspirated
ग	g	as in big
घ	gh	*g* above aspirated
ङ	ṅ	like *ng* in wing
च	c	like *ch* in rich
छ	ch	*c* above aspirated
ज	j	as in joy
झ	jh	*j* above aspirated

ञ	ñ	like *n* in inch
ट	ṭ	like *t* in it
ठ	ṭh	*t* above aspirated
ड	ḍ	like *d* in lid
ढ	ḍh	*d* above aspirated
ण	ṇ	like *n* in under
त	t	like in thin (pronounced gently)
थ	th	*t* above aspirated
द	d	like *th* in then (pronounced gently)
ध	dh	*d* above aspirated
न	n	like *n* in moon
प	p	like *p* in cup
फ	ph	*p* above aspirated
ब	b	like *b* in nib
भ	bh	*b* above aspirated
म	m	like *m* in name
य	y	like *y* in you
र	r	like *r* in car
ल	l	like *l* in call
व	v	like *v* in cave

श	ś	between *s* and *sh* as in Śaṅkara Śiva
ष	ṣ	*sh* as in bush
स	s	like *s* in bus
ह	h	like *h* in hand
ं	ṁ	see notes on transliteration
ः	ḥ	see notes on transliteration

First Edition
1993

॥ श्रीः ॥

॥ निर्गुणमानसपूजा ॥

Nirguṇa Mānasa Pūja

Worship of the Attributeless One in the Mind

Verse 1

शिष्य उवाच–

अखण्डे सच्चिदानन्दे
निर्विकल्पैकरूपिणि ।
स्थितेऽद्वितीयभावेऽपि
कथं पूजा विधीयते ॥ १ ॥

ŚIṢYA UVĀCA:

AKHAṆDE SAC-CHID-ĀNANDE
NIRVIKALPAIKA-RŪPIṆI
STHITE'DVITĪYA BHĀVE-PI
KATHAM PŪJA VIDHĪYATE

śiṣya uvāca:	The disciple said:
akhaṇde	in the undivided
sacchidānande	in the Existence–Consciousness–Bliss
nirvikalpa-eka-rūpini	in the One nature devoid of misconceptions
sthite-advitiya-bhave-api	even when remaining in the non-dual state
katham-pūja-vidhīyate	how is worship prescribed?

The disciple asked:

What manner of worship is prescribed for the One existing as undivided Being-Consciousness-Bliss with no second, without misconceptions, and of one nature?

Verse 2

पूर्णस्यावाहनं कुत्र
सर्वाधारस्य चासनम् ।
स्वच्छस्य पाद्यमर्घ्यं च
शुद्धस्याचमनं कुतः ॥ २ ॥

PŪRṆASY-ĀVĀHANAṀ KUTRA
SARVĀ-DHĀRASYA CĀ-SANAM
SVACCHASYA PĀDYAM-ARGHYAṀ CA
ŚUDDHASY-ĀCAMANAṀ KUTAḤ

pūrṇasya-āvāhanam-kutra	where (is to be done) the invocation of the perfect and complete
sarva-ādhārasya-ca-āsanam	and (where) the seat for the one who is the support of all
svacchasya	for the one who is pure, transparent,
pādyam-arghyam-ca	water for feet washing and respectful libation
śuddhasya-ācamanam-kutaḥ	wherefore the sips of water for the pure one

In what manner is the invocation (āvāhana) to be done for the full and perfect One, and what is the seat (āsana) to be offered for one who is the support of all? And wherefore the water for washing the feet (pādya) and the respectful oblation (arghya) as also the sips of water (āchamana) for the immaculate?

Verse 3

निर्मलस्य कुतः स्नानं
वासो विश्वोदरस्य च ।
अगोत्रस्य त्ववर्णस्य
कुतस्तस्योपवीतकम् ॥ ३ ॥

NIRMALASYA KUTAḤ SNĀNAṀ
VĀSO VIŚVO-DARASYA CA
AGOTRASYA TVA-VARṆASYA
KUTAS-TAS-YOPAVĪTAKAM

nirmalasya	for the spotless
kutaḥ-snānam	wherefore the bath
vāsaḥ-viśva-udarasya-ca	and garments for one who holds the universe in his belly
agotrasya tu-	for one without a lineage, indeed
avarṇasya	for one without a caste
kutaḥ-tasya-upavītakam	wherefore, for him, the sacred thread

Wherefore is the ablution (snāna) for the spotless and the garment (vastra) for one who has the universe in his belly? Wherefore are the triple strands of sacred thread (upavita) for one who has no family lineage from rishis (gotra) and no caste?

Verse 4

निर्लेपस्य कुतो गन्धः
पुष्पं निर्वासनस्य च ।
निर्विशेषस्य का भूषा
कोऽलंकारो निराकृतेः ॥ ४ ॥

NIRLEPASYA KUTO GANDHAḤ
PUṢPAṀ NIR-VĀSANASYA CA
NIR-VIŚEṢASYA KĀ BHŪṢĀ
KO'LAṄKĀRO NIR-ĀKṚTEḤ

nirlepasya	for the stainless (unanointed)
kutaḥ - gandhaḥ	wherefore the sandal (paste) (to anoint)
puṣpam ca	and flowers
nirvāsanasya	for one without scents (of the past)
nirviśesaṣya	for one without any distinguishing features
kā - bhūṣā	what (the) adornment
kaḥ - alankāraḥ - nirākṛteḥ	what beautification for the formless

Wherefore are the sandal paste (candana) for one free from anointments and flowers (puṣpa) for one free of vasanas? What is the adornment (ābharaṇa) for one without distinguishing features; what is the beautification for the formless?

Verse 5

निरञ्जनस्य किं धुपै-
दीपैर्वा सर्वसाक्षिणः ।
निजानन्दैकतृप्तस्य
नैवेद्यं किं भवेदिह ॥ ५ ॥

NIR-AÑJANASYA KIṀ DHŪPAIR-
DĪPAIR-VĀ SARVA SĀKṢIṆAḤ
NIJĀNANDAIKA-TṚPTASYA
NAIVEDYAṀ KIṀ BHAVED-IHA

niranjanasya	for the untainted
kim-dhūpaiḥ	what (of) incense
dīpaiḥ-vā	or of lights
sarva-sākṣiṇaḥ	for the witness of all
nija-ānanda-eka-tṛptasya	for one satisfied in his own bliss
naivedyam-kim-bhaved-iha	what shall be the food offering here

What is the need of waving incense (dhūpa) before the taintless and of waving light (dīpa) for one who is the Witness of all? What shall be the cooked food (naivedya) for one who is completely satisfied with his own Bliss?

Verse 6

विश्वानन्दयितुस्तस्य
किं ताम्बूलं प्रकल्पते ।
स्वयंप्रकाशचिद्रूपो
योऽसावर्कादिभासकः ॥ ६ ॥

VIŚVĀNANDA-YITUS-TASYA
KIṀ TĀMBŪLAṀ PRAKALPATE
SVAYAṀ-PRAKĀŚA-CID-RUPO
YO'SĀV-ARKĀDI-BHĀSAKAḤ

viśva-ānandayituḥ-tasya	for him who makes the universe happy
kim-tāmbulam-prakalpate	what betel pack is considered proper
svayam-prakāśa	one who is self-luminous
cid-rūpaḥ	of the nature of Consciousness
yah-asau	he who
arka-ādi-bhāsakaḥ	is the illuminator of the sun and such

What is designated as the betel leaves (tāmbūla) for one who makes the universe joyous? For one who is self-luminous and all-consciousness and is the illuminator of the sun and other luminaries,

Verse 7

गीयते श्रुतिभिस्तस्य
नीराजनविधिः कुतः ।
प्रदक्षिणमनन्तस्य
प्रमाणोऽद्वयवस्तुनः ॥ ७ ॥

GĪYATE ŚRUTIBHIS-TASYA
NĪRĀJANA VIDHIḤ KUTAḤ
PRADAKṢIṆAM-ANANTASYA
PRAMĀṆO'DVAYA VASTUNAḤ

gīyate-śrutibhiḥ-tasya	for him who is glorified by the Vedas
nīrājana-vidhiḥ-kutaḥ	wherefore the ritual of camphor-waving
pradaksiṇàm-anantasya	(and) circumambulation for the limitless
pramāṇah-advaya-vastunaḥ	(who is) the proof of the non-dual reality

what is the mode of camphor light offering (nīrajāna) for one who is glorified by the Vedas? Wherefore is the circumambulation (pradakṣina) of the one who is endless and is the proof of non-dual Truth?

VERSE 8

वेदवाचामवेद्यस्य
किं वा स्तोत्रं विधीयते ।
अन्तर्बहिः संस्थित-
स्योद्वासनविधिः कुतः ॥ ८ ॥

VEDA-VĀCĀM-AVEDYASYA
KIṀ VĀ STOTRAṀ VIDHĪYATE
ANTAR-BAHIḤ SAM-STHITASYA
UDVĀSANA VIDHIḤ KUTAḤ

veda-vācām-avedyasya	for one who cannot be comprehended by the words of the Vedas
kim-vā-stotram-vidhīyate	what indeed is the eulogy prescribed
antaḥ-bahiḥ-saṃsthitasya	for one who is established both inside and outside
udvāsana-vidhiḥ-kutaḥ	wherefore the ritual of sending away (after leave-taking) after worship

What is the song of praise (stotra) prescribed for praising the One beyond understanding through the words of the Vedas? What is the way of bidding a good-bye (udvāsana) to One who exists both inside and outside?

Verse 9

श्रीगुरुरुवाच-

आराधयामि मणिसंनिभमात्मलिङ्गं
मायापुरीहृदयपङ्कजसंनिविष्टम् ।
श्रद्धानदीविमलचित्तजलाभिषेकै-
र्नित्यं समाधिकुसुमैरपुनर्भवाय ॥ ९ ॥

ŚRĪ GURUR-UVĀCA:

ĀRĀDHAYĀMI MAṆI-SANNIBHAM-ĀTMA-LINGAṀ
MĀYĀ PURĪ HṚDAYA PAṄKAJA SANNIVIṢṬAM
ŚRADDHĀ-NADĪ-VIMALA-CITTA-JALĀBHIṢEKAIR-
NITYAM SAMĀDHI-KUSUMAIR-APUNAR-BHĀVAYA

śri guruḥ uvāca:	the revered Guru said (replied):
ārādhāyami	I worship
mani-sannibham	the bejewelled
ātma-liṅgam	linga of the Self
māyāpurī-hrdaya-	seated in the city of maya or the heart-lotus of the
paṅkaja-sanniviṣtam	illusory body
śraddhā-nadī-vimala-citta	by ablutions (abhiṣeka) in the clear water of thought
jala-abhiṣekaiḥ	in the river of faith
nityam	always (daily, ever)
samādhi-kusumaiḥ-	by the flowers of samadhi
a-punar-bhavāya	for not being born again

The revered Guru replied:

I worship the bejewelled linga of the Self (Ātmalinga), residing in the city of maya, the lotus of the heart of the illusory body, by the sacred ablution and anointing (abhiṣeka) of the clear water of thought (citta) in the river of faith (śraddha) and by the flowers of samādhi for not being born again.

Verse 10

अयमेकोऽवशिष्टोऽस्मी-
त्येवमावाहयेच्छिवम् ।
आसनं कल्पयेत्पश्चा-
त्स्वप्रतिष्ठात्मचिन्तनम् ॥ १० ॥

AYAM EKO'VAŚIṢṬO-SMĪT-
YEVAM-ĀVĀHAYEC-CHIVAṀ
ĀSANAM KALPAYET-PAŚCAT-
SVA-PRATIṢṬH-ĀTMA-CINTANAM

ayam ekaḥ	this one (alone) (I)
avaśiṣtaḥ asmi	am the remaining
iti-evam-āvāhayet-śivam	thus indeed should Śiva be invoked (avahanam)
āsanam kalpayet	the seat (āsanam) should then be formed
paścāt	thereafter
sva-pratistha-	(which is) the thought of the Self being
ātma-cintanam	established in oneself

I am the only one remaining—thus is Śiva to be invoked. Then the thought of the Self established in oneself should be offered as the seat (āsana).

Verse 11

पुण्यपापरजःसङ्गो
मम नास्तीति वेदनम् ।
पाद्यं समर्पयेद्विद्वा-
न्सर्वकल्मषनाशनम् ॥ ११ ॥

PUṆYA-PĀPA-RAJAS-SAṄGO
MAMA NĀSTĪ-TI VEDANAṀ
PĀDYAM SAMARPAYED-VIDVĀN-
SARVA-KALMAṢA-NĀŚANAM

puṇya pāpa rajaḥ sangaḥ	connection to the dust of sin and good merit
mama nāsti	is not for me
iti vedanam	a perception thus
pādyam samarpayet vidvān	the learned one should offer (as) water for feet-washing (pādya)
sarva-kalmaṣa-nāśanam	which does away with all impurities

There is no connection for me with the dust of merit or demerit (puṇya or pāpa)—perceiving thus, the learned one should offer water for washing of the feet (pādya) that will wash off all impurities.

Verse 12

अनादिकल्पविधृत-
मूलाज्ञानजलाञ्जलिम् ।
विसृजेदात्मलिङ्गस्य
तदेवार्घ्यसमर्पणम् ॥ १२ ॥

ANĀDI-KALPA-VIDHṚTA
MŪLĀJÑĀNA JALĀÑJALIṀ
VISṚJED-ĀTMA-LIṄGASYA
TADEV-ĀRGHYA-SAMARPANAṀ

anādi-kalpa-vidhṛtam	carried practically originless
mūla-ajnāna-	the primal ignorance
jalāṇjalim-visṛjet	(as) the salutation with water, should be poured down
ātma-liṅgasya	on the linga of the Self
tad-eva	that indeed
arghya-samarpaṇam	is the offering of respectful libation (arghyam)

Pouring of the water of primal ignorance that is originless and has continued for aeons on the linga of the Self is indeed the offering of the respectful libation (arghya).

Verse 13

ब्रह्मानन्दाब्धिकल्लोल-
कणकोठ्यंशलेशकम् ।
पिबन्तीन्द्रादय इति
ध्यानमाचमनं मतम् ॥ १३ ॥

BRAHMĀNAND-ĀBDHI-KALLOLA
KAṆAKOṬ-YAMŚA LEŚAKAṀ
PIBANT-ĪNDRĀDAYA ITI
DHYĀNAM-ĀCAMANAṀ MATAM

brahma-ānanda-abdhi-kallola	(of) a wave in the ocean of Brahman-bliss
kaṇa-koṭi-amśa-leśakam	the slightest part of a particle of a millionth part of a drop
pibanti-indrādaya	Indra, (the chief of gods) and others drink (enjoy)
iti ācamanam matam	this is considered the offering of sips of water (ācamanam)

The meditation that Indra and others drink of only a tiny drop of a millionth part of the billows of the ocean of Brahman-Bliss is understood to be the sips of water (ācamana).

Verse 14

ब्रह्मानन्दजलेनैव
लोकाः सर्वे परिप्लुताः ।
अच्छेद्योऽयमिति ध्यान-
मभिषेचनमात्मनः ॥ १४ ॥

BRAHMĀNANDA-JALENAIVA
LOKĀḤ SARVE PARI-PLUTĀḤ
ACCHEDYO'YAM-ITI DHYĀNAM-
ABHIṢECANAM-ĀTMANAḤ

brahma-ānanda-jalena-eva	indeed by the waters of the Brahman-bliss
lokāh sarve	all the worlds
pariplutāḥ	are flooded
acchedyaḥ ayam	this is indivisible
iti dhyānam	a meditation thus
abhiṣecanam ātmanaḥ	(is) the abhiṣeka (ablution/anointing) for the Self

All the worlds are, indeed, flooded with the waters of Brahman-Bliss. The meditation that I am indivisible is the sacred ablution and anointing (abhiṣeka) for the Self.

VERSE 15

निरावरणचैतन्यं
प्रकाशोऽस्मीति चिन्तनम् ।
आत्मलिङ्गस्य सद्वस्त्र-
मित्येवं चिन्तयेन्मुनिः ॥ १५ ॥

NIR-ĀVARAṆA-CAITANYAṀ
PRAKAŚO'SMĪ-TI CINTANAṀ
ĀTMA-LINGASYA SAD-VASTRAM-
IT.YEVAṀ CINTAYEN-MUNIḤ

nir-āvarana-caitanyam	(I am) the sentience without any veiling
prakāśah-asmi	(I am) radiant, (effulgent), (shining), (luminous)
iti cintanam	thinking thus
ātmalingasya sad-vastram	is the true garment (vastram) for the linga of the Self
iti evam cintayet muniḥ	the Sage should indeed reflect thus

I am the light of the veil-less Consciousness. This is the true draping (vastra) for the Ātmalinga. Thus should the Sage reflect.

Verse 16

त्रिगुणात्माशेषलोक-
मालिकासूत्रमस्म्यहम् ।
इति निश्चयमेवात्र-
ह्युपवीतं परं मतम् ॥ १६ ॥

TRI-GUṆĀTMĀ-ŚESA-LOKA
MALIKĀ-SŪTRAM-ASMYAHAṀ
ITI NIŚCAYAM-EVĀTRA
HY-UPAVĪTAM PARAṀ MATAṀ

tri-guṇa-ātma	comprising of the triple strands (guṇa–s)
aśeṣa-loka-mālikā	of the garland of worlds without end
sūtram asmi aham	I am the thread that runs through (sūtram)
iti niścayam evatra	a certitude thus indeed
upavītam paraṃ matam	is considered the supreme sacred thread (upavītam)

The certitude that I am the thread that runs through the garlands of the entire world of the triple strands of qualities is, indeed, here understood to be the Supreme triple strand of sacred thread (upavīta).

Verse 17

अनेकवासनामिश्र-
प्रपञ्चोऽयं धृतो मया ।
नान्येनेत्यनुसंधान-
मात्मनश्चन्दनं भवेत् ॥ १७ ॥

ANEKA-VĀSANĀ-MIŚRA-
PRAPAÑCO'YAṀ DHṚTO MAYĀ
NĀNYENETY-ANU-SANDHĀNAM-
ĀTMANAŚ-CANDANAṀ BHAVET

aneka-vāsanā-miśraḥ-	this manifest world with mixture of numerous
prapancaḥ-ayam	scents (vasanas)
dhṛtam mayā	is supported by me
na anyena	not by anyone else
iti anusandhānam	an inquiry, thus
ātmanaḥ candanam bhavet	will be the (fragrant) sandal paste for the Self

The reflection that this phenomenal world composed of numerous mixed vasanas (scents; tendencies) is held by me and by none else will be the sandal paste (candana) for the Self.

VERSE 18

रजःसत्त्वतमोवृत्ति-
त्यागरूपैस्तिलाक्षतैः ।
आत्मलिङ्गं यजेन्नित्यं
जीवन्मुक्तिप्रसिद्धये ॥ १८ ॥

RAJAS-SATVA-TAMO-VṚTTI-
TYĀGA-RŪPAIS-TIL-ĀKṢATAIḤ
ĀTMA-LINGAṀ YAJEN-NITYAṀ
JĪVAN-MUKTI-PRASIDDHAYE

rajaḥ-sattvaḥ-tamaḥ-vritti tyāga-rūpaih	in the form of the renunciation of the modes of the equiposed, the energetic and the dull (sattva, rajas, tamas)
tila-akṣataiḥ	(by such) sesame and rice grains
ātma-lingam yajet nityam	the linga of the Self should be worshipped ever
jīvan-mukti prasiddhaye	for attaining liberation while yet in body

With the abandonment of the diverse modes of raja's, sattva, and tamas, as sesame seeds (tila) and unbroken rice grains (akṣata), the Linga of the Self should be worshipped for the full attainment of jivanmukti.

Verse 19

ईश्वरो गुरुरात्मेति
भेदत्रयविवर्जितैः ।
बिल्वपत्रैरद्वितीयै-
रात्मलिङ्गं यजेच्छिवम् ॥ १९ ॥

ĪŚVARO GURUR-ĀTMETI
BHEDA-TRAYA-VIVARJITAIḤ
BILVA-PATRAIR-ADVĪTIYAIR-
ĀTMA-LINGAṀ YAJEC-CHIVAM

īśvaraḥ-guruḥ-ātmā-iti	Isvara, Guru and the Self—devoid of a
bheda-traya-vivarjitaiḥ	threefold difference thus
bilva patraiḥ	by means of (such) bilva leaves (sacred to Śiva)
advitīyaiḥ	of non-duality
ātma-lingam yajet śivam	one should worship the peaceful, auspicious linga of the Self

One should worship the auspicious, peaceful linga of the Self with bilva leaves that are the abandonment of the triple differentiation of Isvara, Guru, and Atma with nothing else as second thereto.

VERSE 20

समस्तवासनात्यागं
धूपं तस्य विचिन्तयेत् ।
ज्योतिर्मयात्मविज्ञानं
दीपं संदर्शयेद्बुधः ॥ २० ॥

SAMASTA-VĀSANĀ-TYĀGAṀ
DHŪPAṀ TASYA VICINTAYET
JYOTIR-MAY-ĀTMA-VIJÑĀNAM
DĪPAṀ SANDARŚAYED-BUDAḤ

samasta-vāsanā-tyāgam	the renunciation of all (past) scents
dhūpam	(fragrant) incense offering
tasya	for him
vicintayet	one should think of
jyotiḥ-maya	full of light
ātma-vijnānam	the knowledge of the Self
dīpam	the offering of the lighted wick
saṁdarśayet bhudaḥ	the wise one should show (wave in front)

The renunciation of vasanas should be thought of as the incense offering to Him. The wise one should wave the light (dīpa) of the luminous Knowledge of the Self.

Verse 21

नैवेद्यमात्मलिङ्गस्य
ब्रह्माण्डाख्यं महोदनम् ।
पिबानन्दरसं स्वादु
मृत्युरस्योपसेचनम् ॥ २१ ॥

NAIVEDYAM-ĀTMA-LINGASYA
BRAHMĀṆḌ-ĀKHYAM MAHODANAṀ
PIB-ĀNANDA-RASAṀ SVĀDU
MṚTYUR-ASY-OPASECANAM

naivedyam-ātma-lingasya	the food offering for the linga of the Self
brahma-aṇḍa-ākhyam-	(is) the massive cooked food (offering)
mahodanam	known as the Cosmic Brahman egg
piba-ānanda-rasam-svādu	the essence of bliss is the relishable drink
mṛtyuh-asya-upasecanam	death (itself) is (but) a condiment for this

The massive cooked rice offering (naivedya) for the Ātmalinga is the cosmos known as the Brahman-egg. The essence of Bliss is the sweet relishable drink. Death itself is but the condiment to go with this cooked food.

Verse 22

अज्ञानोच्छिष्टकरस्य
क्षालनं ज्ञानवारिणा ।
विशुद्धस्यात्मलिङ्गस्य
हस्तप्रक्षालनं स्मरेत् ॥ २२ ॥

AJÑĀNO-CCHIṢṬA-KARASYA
KṢĀLANAṀ JÑĀNA-VĀRIṆĀ
VIŚUDDHASY-ĀTMA-LINGASYA
HASTA-PRAKṢĀLANAṀ SMARET

ajnāna-ucchiṣta-karasya	for the hand that is the polluted remains of ignorance
kṣālaṇam-jnāna-vāriṇā	washing by the waters of knowledge
viśuddhasya-ātma-lingasya	for the pure linga of the Self
hasta-prakṣālanam-smaret	should be remembered (thought of, construed) as the hand washing

One should remember the hand washing (hasta prakṣalana) of the pure Ātmalinga as the washing of the hand polluted with the remains of ignorance (ajñana) with the water of Knowledge.

Verse 23

रागादिगुणशून्यस्य
शिवस्य परमात्मनः ।
सरागविषयाभ्यास-
त्यागस्ताम्बूलचर्वणम् ॥ २३ ॥

RĀGĀDI-GUṆA-ŚŪNYASYA
ŚIVASYA PARAMĀTMANAḤ
SA-RĀGA-VIṢAY-ĀBHYĀSA-
TYĀGAS-TĀMBŪLA-CARVAṆAM

rāga-ādi-guṇa-sūnyasya	for one devoid of the qualities such as passion (attachment) and others
śivāsya paramātmanaḥ	for Śiva the Supreme Self
sa-rāga-viṣaya-abhyāsa-tyāgaḥ	the renunciation of the practice of passion (attachment) for objects
tāmbūla carvaṇam	is the chewing of betel packs

The offering of betels (tāmbūla), for chewing, to the Supreme Self, Śiva, devoid of attachment and other qualities, is the sacrifice of the practice of attachment to things.

VERSE 24

अज्ञानध्वान्तविध्वंस-
प्रचण्डमतिभास्करम् ।
आत्मनो ब्रह्मताज्ञानं
नीराजनमिहात्मनः ॥ २४ ॥

AJÑĀNA-DHVĀNTA-VIDHVAMSA-
PRACAṆḌA-MĀTI-BHĀSKARAṀ
ĀTMANO BRAHMATĀ-JÑĀNAṀ
NĪRĀJANAM-IHĀTMANAḤ

ajnāna-dhvānta-vidhvamsa	wiping off the darkness of ignorance
pracaṇḍa-mati-bhāskaram	the powerful illuminating (sun of) intellect
ātmanaḥ brahmatā jnānam	the knowledge of the Atman being Brahman (the knowledge of oneself being Brahman)
nīrājanam-iha-ātmanaḥ	(is) here the waving of camphor light for the Self

The camphor light offering (nirājana) to the Self, here, is one's own Knowledge of Brahmanhood. That, like the dazzling sun, destroys the darkness of ignorance (ajñana).

Verse 25

विविधब्रह्मसंदृष्टि-
मालिकाभिरलंकृतम् ।
पूर्णानन्दात्मतादृष्टिं
पुष्पाञ्जलिमनुस्मरेत् ॥ २५ ॥

VIVIDHA ḄRAHMA SANDṚṢṬIR-
MĀLIKĀBIR-ALAṄKṚTAM
PŪRṆĀNAND-ĀTMATĀ-DṚṢṬIM
PUṢPĀÑJALIM-ANUSMARET

vividha-brahma-saṁdṛṣṭiḥ-	adorned by the garlands of the perception of
mālikabhiḥ-alaṅkṛtam	Brahman in different manifestations
pūrṇa-ānanda-ātmatā-dṛṣṭim	the perception of the Self as the perfect bliss
puṣpāñjalim-anusmaret	should be exclusively remembered as the offering of flowers

One should remember the perception of Brahman in multifarious forms as the adornment with garlands (mala-ābharaṇa) and the perception of the Self as full and perfect Bliss as the scattering of flowers (puṣpanjali).

VERSE 26

परिभ्रमन्ति ब्रह्माण्ड-
सहस्राणि मयीश्वरे ।
कूटस्थाचलरूपोऽह-
मिति ध्यानं प्रदक्षिणम् ॥ २६ ॥

PARI-BHRAMANTĪ BRAHMĀṆḌA
SAHASRĀṆI MAY-ĪŚVARE
KŪTASTH-ĀCHALA RŪPO'HAM-
ITI DHYĀNAṀ PRADAKṢINAM

paribhramanti-brahma-aṇḍa-sahasrāṇi	millions of brahman eggs (universes) revolve
mayi īśvare	in me, the Isvara
kūtastha-acala-rūpaḥ-aham	I am of the nature of the Supreme, unmoving (like an anvil), immovable
iti-dhyānam-pradakṣiṇam	meditation thus is the circumambulation

Millions of universes wander inside me, Isvara. I am the unmovable and motionless nature—this contemplation is the circumambulation (pradakṣina).

VERSE 27

विश्ववन्द्योऽहमेवास्मि
नास्ति वन्द्यो मदन्यतः ।
इत्यालोचनमेवात्र
स्वात्मलिङ्गस्य वन्दनम् ॥ २७ ॥

VISVA-VANDYO'HAM-EVĀSMI
NĀSTI VANDYO MADANYATAḤ
ITY-ĀLOCANAM-EVĀTRA
SVĀTMA-LINGASYA VANDANAM

viśva-vandyaḥ-aham-eva-asmi	I indeed am the one to whom all the universe should make obeisance
na-asti-vandyaḥ	none there is to be bowed to
mad-anyataḥ	apart from me
iti ālocanam eva atra	reflecting thus indeed here
su-ātma-lingasya-vandanam	is the obeisance to the excellent (exalted) linga of the Self

I, alone am the One to whom the universe should make obeisance (namaskāra). There is none else to whom to bow—thinking thus is, indeed, the salutation to the Ātmalinga.

Verse 28

आत्मनः सत्क्रिया प्रोक्ता
कर्तव्याभावभावना ।
नामरूपव्यतीतात्म-
चिन्तनं नामकीर्तनम् ॥ २८ ॥

ĀTMANAḤ SAT-KRIYĀ PROKTĀ
KARTAVY-ĀBHĀVA-BHĀVANĀ
NĀMA-RŪPA-VYATĪT-ĀTMA-
CINTANAṀ NĀMA-KĪRTANAM

ātmanaḥ sat-kriyā prokta	the true activity of the Self is said to be
kartavya-abhāva-bhāvanam	the bhava (conviction, attitude) that nothing exists to be done
nāma-rūpa-vyatīta	transcending name and form
ātma-cintanam	the thought (understanding) of the Self
nāma-kīrtanam	(is) the singing of the names

The conviction about nonaction is said to be the true activity of the Self. The thought of the Self transcending names and forms is, indeed, the singing of the names in worship (nāma kīrtana).

Verse 29

श्रवणं तस्य देवस्य
श्रोतव्याभावचिन्तनम् ।
मननं त्वात्मलिङ्गस्य
मन्तव्याभावचिन्तनम् ॥ २९ ॥

ŚRAVAṆAṀ TASYA DEVASYA
ŚROTAVY-ĀBHĀVA-CINTANAṀ
MANANAṀ T-VĀTMA-LIṄGASYA
MANTAVY-ĀBHĀVA-CINTANAM

śravaṇam tasya devasya	listening to that Lord
srotavya-abhāva-cintanam	is the thought (understanding) of the non-existence of anything to be heard
mananam-tu-ātma-lingasya	the mental reflection of the linga of the Self, too
mantavya-abhāva-cintanam	(is) the thought (understanding) of the non-existence of anything to be reflected upon

Listening (śravaṇa) to that deva (deity) is the understanding that the heard is non-existent. Reflection (manana) on the Ātmalinga is the understanding that there is nothing upon which to reflect.

VERSE 30

ध्यातव्याभावविज्ञानमं
निदिध्यासनमात्मनः ।
समस्तभ्रान्तिविक्षेप-
राहित्येनात्मनिष्ठता ॥ ३० ॥

DHYĀTAVY-ĀBHĀVA-VIJÑĀNAṀ
NIDIDHYĀSANAM-ĀTMANAḤ
SAMASTA-BHRĀNTI-VIKṢEPA-
RĀHITYEN-ĀTMA-NIṢṬHATĀ

dhyātavya-abhāva-vijnānam	the knowledge of the non-existence of anything to be meditated upon
nididhyāsanam-ātmanaḥ	is the profound meditation on the Self
samasta-bhrānti-vikṣepa-rāhityena	by the freedom from false projection of all mental errors
ātma-niṣṭhatā	(is) the abidance in the Self

The Knowledge of the non-existence of anything upon which to meditate is the profound meditation on the Self. Abidance in the Self is to be free of all errors and misconceptions.

VERSE 31

समाधिरात्मनो नाम
नान्यच्चित्तस्य विभ्रमः ।
तत्रैव ब्रह्मणि सदा
चित्तविश्रान्तिरिष्यते ॥ ३१ ॥

SAMĀDHIR-ĀTMANO NĀMA
NĀNYAC-CITTASYA VIBHRAMAḤ
TATRAIVA BRAHMAṆI SADĀ
CITTA-VIŚRĀNTIR-IṢYATE

samādhiḥ-ātmanaḥ-nāma	what is named the samadhi in the Self
na-anyat-cittasya-vibhramaḥ	is the absence of mental error of anything else (existing)
tatra-eva-brahmaṇi-sadā	there also, always (abiding) in Brahman
citta-viśrāntiḥ-iṣyate	is laid down (prescribed) as repose of thought

What is named the samadhi of the Self is the absence of the hallucinations of the mind of anything else as existent. There, itself, repose of the mind is declared to be abidance in Brahman.

VERSE 32

एवं वेदान्तकल्पोक्त
स्वात्मलिङ्गप्रपूजनम् ।
कुर्वन्ना मरणं वापि
क्षणं वा सुसमाहितः ॥ ३२ ॥

EVAM VEDĀNTA KALPOKTA
SVĀTMA-LIṄGA PRA-PŪJANAṀ
KURVANN-Ā MARAṆAṀ VĀPI
KṢANAṀ VĀ SUSAMĀHITAḤ

evam-vedānta-kalpa-ukta	thus, as spoken of in Vedantic canon,
su-ātma-linga-	performing the worship of the linga of one's
prapūjanam-kurvan	own Self (of the exalted linga of the Self)
ā-maranam-kṣanam-vā-api	until death, or even for a moment
su-samāhitaḥ	extremely calm and collected

Thus, performing the worship of the Ātmalinga according to the canons of Vedanta, all through life until death or for just a moment, with full composure,

Verse 33

सर्वदुर्वासनाजालं
पदपांसुमिव त्यजेत् ।
विधूयाज्ञानदुःखौघं
मोक्षानन्दं समश्नुते ॥ ३३ ॥

SARVA-DURVĀSANĀ-JĀLAṀ
PADA-PĀMSUM-IVA TYAJET
VIDHŪY-ĀJÑĀNA-DUHKH-AUGHAṀ
MOKṢĀNANDAṀ SAMAŚNUTE

sarva-durvāsanā-jālam	the tangled web of all (past) bad tendencies (durvasana)
pada-pāmsum-iva-tyajet	one should renounce like the dust of the feet
vidhūya-ajnāna-duhkha-	cutting (shaking) off the stream of the
ogham	sorrow of ignorance
mokṣa-ānandam-samaśnute	one enjoys (savors) well, the bliss of liberation

one should renounce the entire network of bad vasanas like the dust on the feet. Shaking off the sorrow-ridden stream of ignorance (ājñāṇa), one savors the Bliss of Liberation.

इति श्रीमच्छंकरभगवतः कृतौ
निर्गुणमानसपूजा संपूर्णा ॥

ITI SRĪMAD ŚANKARA
BHAGAVATAḤ KṚTAU
NIRGUṆA MĀNASA PŪJA
SAMPŪRṆĀ

Thus, Srimad Śaṅkara Bhagavan's

Nirguṇa Mānasa Pūja

concluded.

Appendix

Upachara-s in Worship (Courtesies and Honors in Pūja)

There are several courtesies and honors accorded to the deity in a pūja or ritual worship. The numbers vary from about five to sixty-four and more according to the tradition practiced and details of worship. The same are extended mentally in mental worship. The various items dealt with in this text are:

Meditation	*(dhyāna)*
Invocation (in the icon or picture or otherwise)	*(āvāhana)*
Offering of seat	*(āsana)*
Water for feet washing	*(padya)*
Respectful libation	*(arghya)*
Sips of water	*(ācamana)*
Formal ablution	*(snāna)*
Garments	*(vastra)*
Triple strand of sacred thread (over left shoulder and under right arm)	*(upavīta)*
Ornaments	*(ābharaṇa)*

Sandal paste	*(candana)*
Rice grains–unbroken	*(akṣata)*
Flowers	*(puṣpa)*
Incense	*(dhūpa)*
Light on a wick	*(dīpa)*
Cooked food	*(naivedya)*
Seasonings	*(upasecanam)*
Water for hand washing	*(hasta praksalana)*
Betel leaves	*(tāmbūla)*
Scattering of flowers	*(puṣpāñjali)*
Waving of camphor light	*(nīrājana)*
Circumambulation (clockwise)	*(pradakṣina)*
Prostration	*(namaskāra)*
Singing of names	*(nāma kīrtana)*
Release (bidding good-bye)	*(udvāsana)*

Index